EXISTENTIALIST ETHICS

New Studies in Ethics

Edited by W. D. Hudson

What is involved in judging a person to be moral or immoral, or in calling an action right or wrong? What makes a man good or an action our duty? Such questions as these, which concern the nature and content of morality, have been discussed by philosophers from earliest times and are still live issues today.

Many different types of ethical theory have emerged. New Studies in Ethics meets the need for an up-to-date examination of the main types. This series of monographs covers the whole range of ethical theory from Greek philosophers to the latest developments in contemporary moral philosophy. Each study is complete in itself and the whole series provides a unique treatment of the main philosophical problems in ethics.

A distinguished team of philosophers, drawn from universities in Great Britain, the U.S.A. and Australia, was invited to prepare these studies. They have provided a series of monographs which will prove indispensable to university students of Moral Philosophy, and will interest any intelligent reader.

The Series

H. B. Acton	*Kant's Moral Philosophy*
J. N. Findlay	*Axiological Ethics*
A. G. N. Flew	*Evolutionary Ethics*
Pamela Huby	*Greek Ethics*
W. D. Hudson	*Ethical Intuitionism*
Eugene Kamenka	*Marxism and Ethics*
J. Kemp	*Ethical Naturalism*
D. J. O'Connor	*Aquinas and Natural Law*
Anthony Quinton	*Utilitarian Ethics*
W. H. Walsh	*Hegelian Ethics*
Mary Warnock	*Existentialist Ethics*
G. J. Warnock	*Contemporary Moral Philosophy*

Existentialist Ethics

MARY WARNOCK, M.A., B.Phil.
Talbot Research Fellow, Lady Margaret Hall, Oxford

MACMILLAN

First editon 1967
Reprinted 1967, 1969, 1970, 1974

Published by
THE MACMILLAN PRESS LTD
London and Basingstoke
Associated companies in New York Dublin
Melbourne Johannesburg and Madras

SBN 333 01178 3

Printed in Great Britain by
THE ANCHOR PRESS LTD
Tiptree, Essex

CONTENTS

EDITOR'S PREFACE

New Studies in Ethics is a series of monographs written by philosophers drawn from universities in Great Britain, the United States and Australia. These studies are analytical and critical, and the series, when complete, will cover the main types of ethical theory from the Greeks to the present day.

The Existentialist authors, with whom the present study is concerned, do not always make easy reading, but Mrs. Warnock has provided an admirably clear guide to their thought. She writes, not unsympathetically, about Kierkegaard, Heidegger and Sartre, and helps us to understand the part which key-concepts, such as freedom and subjectivity, have played in their philosophy. The manner in which they discuss ethical problems and the kind of conclusions at which they arrive are illustrated. Weaknesses in Existentialist moral philosophy are exposed and an attempt made to assess the advantages and disadvantages of this approach to ethics.

The authors here discussed have had a very wide influence. Not only have their ideas of human nature and activity been the inspiration of many modern novelists and playwrights; but they constitute one of the sources of the 'Situational Ethics' which some religious thinkers are now advocating. Mrs. Warnock's study furnishes all who are interested in such matters, as well as students of moral philosophy, with a brief, but penetrating, introduction to Existentialist Ethics.

W. D. HUDSON

I. INTRODUCTION

Anyone writing about Existentialism ought perhaps to begin by trying to define what is being discussed. Yet one may well feel apologetic for attempting yet another definition of this particular term, since the books on the subject are innumerable, and there is not one of them that does not start with an attempt at a new definition. This is understandable, for there are grave difficulties in the way of reaching a satisfactory account of the matter. In the body of philosophical writing which could reasonably be called Existentialist, there is a whole number of contrary tendencies, and trying to reduce these to order is apt to lead to no more than an historical account of the whole Existentialist trend in philosophy, starting with Socrates. On the other hand, if one tries to extract the salient point of Existentialism by concentrating on the official statement of its central concept, namely the belief that *existence precedes essence*, then this does not advance one very far. For the belief itself is not readily intelligible, and in any case it has little point except in the context of the complete system of Sartre's philosophy. But Sartre cannot be thought to have been the only Existentialist, even though he was the most systematic. (I write of him in the past since, as we shall see, he is not an Existentialist any more.) Other short definitions seem to suffer the same fate. Either they do not make sense, or they apply to only part of the field. I shall, therefore, abandon the attempt to define Existentialism.

Nevertheless, one must not exaggerate the complexities of the subject. There is, without doubt, such a phenomenon as Existentialist philosophy, and a group of Existentialist philosophers, and it is to the members of this group that I shall now turn. If one has to be content with the discovery of no more than a family resemblance between the members, one may reflect that the same would probably have to content one if the subject were Empiricism, Rationalism, or Idealism. As to the question who is to be included in the group, this too presents difficulties, but, for the present purpose, not important difficulties. For my aim is to try to state what is the *general* ethical standpoint of Existentialism, and with what *common* presuppositions Existentialist philosophers must approach the construction of a moral philosophy; and this can be done without settling the question of the exact boundaries of Existentialism itself. There are some agreed, central, Existentialist writers, and it is enough, for the present purpose, to concentrate attention on some of these. I shall in fact consider only three. First, I shall discuss briefly the work of Søren Kierkegaard (1813–55), who actually invented the term 'Existentialism', and is in many ways properly regarded as the father of the movement. Next will come Martin Heidegger (1889–), particularly his book *Sein und Zeit*, translated as *Being and Time* (London, 1962). Finally, I shall consider at some length the pre-war work of Jean-Paul Sartre (1905–), concentrating mainly on his long book *L'Être et le Néant*, first published in Paris in 1943, and translated into English, as *Being and Nothingness*, by Hazel Barnes (London, 1957).

There is one more general warning which should be given. In the philosophers who are about to be discussed there is no sharp or clear distinction between ethics and the rest of philosophy. They sought, all of them, to get us to see the world in a new light, and if they succeeded, this would no doubt affect, to some extent, the way we behaved, and the way we thought about our own behaviour and that of others, as much as it would affect how we thought about other things. Thus it is sometimes possible to deduce an ethical theory, or something like it, from their philosophy, for it may be possible to say, in their persons, 'This is how you ought to see human conduct'. But, in general, this is all that can be done. All I can hope is that, in the following exposition, the *kind* of ethical outlook that is implicit in Existentialism will emerge. But it must be clearly stated at the outset that what emerges is for the most part something less than a complete ethical theory or system. Nor is it just an accidental feature of the writers in question that in none of them is there to be found a coherent or systematic moral philosophy. To construct such a system would perhaps have been impossible, in the sense that it would have been contrary to the general intention of their work.

The most systematic Existentialist, as I have already said, is J.-P. Sartre, but even he had no properly ethical theory. All the same, most of the present essay is concerned with Sartre, and this perhaps requires some explanation. The first justification is that he is plainly the most influential living philosopher who has ever been willing to be called an Existentialist. (Heidegger, whom I shall consider very briefly, is not willing to be so described. Moreover, except in his own country, his influence has mostly been through the writings of Sartre.) Secondly, there is in Sartre an extraordinary combination of influences at work, and this extreme receptivity to the thought of other philosophers is itself a characteristic of Existentialism. Everything is grist to their mill. Everything is taken over and 'interiorised', in Sartre's word, that is to say, made personal. Thirdly, Sartre has given up Existentialism; and this fact is not irrelevant. For, as I hope to show, it was impossible for him to produce a coherent ethical theory within the confines of Existentialism; and it was partly for this reason, though doubtless also for other more political reasons, that he finally gave up Existentialism for Marxism. By discussing the development of Sartre's thought, then, we may hope to throw some light on the common presuppositions and the necessary limitations of Existentialist thought, in so far as it refers to ethics.

II. KIERKEGAARD

Let us now turn to Søren Kierkegaard. There are in his writings certain ideas which in one form or another recur in all Existentialist writers, and which are crucial in determining the nature of Existentialist ethics, though these ideas are later developed in ways which would be surprising to Kierkegaard himself, and would certainly have been rejected by him. Most obviously, the development of Sartrean Existentialism, its conversion to Marxism, and its final extinction, would have been repulsive to Kierkegaard. But, all the same, there are seeds of even this development in his own work.

What, then, are the features of his work, and indeed of his life, which make it reasonable to think of him as the first Existentialist writer? He was, as a child, deeply affected by the religious gloom and guilt of his father. As a young man he believed himself to have thrown off this influence entirely and to have escaped what seemed like the intolerable chains which had, quite unnecessarily, been imposed on him in his childhood. For a time he devoted himself to observing and enjoying the world, without any commitment either to a faith or to a set of moral principles. In 1836 he underwent a conversion to morality; and two years later he was converted again, this time to Christianity. Each of the stages he went through, as he looked back on them afterwards, seemed, to various degrees, stages of illusion. His freedom after his childhood was illusory (a stage which he called the 'Aesthetic'); his conversion to morality committed him to belief in a kind of universal law absent from the Aesthetic. This was a higher stage, as he later saw it, but could not be the final stage in his development, because it was based on the illusion of 'humanism', or the failure to recognise the existence of the *transcendental* as an element in human life. The conversion to religion was the removal of this illusion, and it was now possible for him to choose to adopt the standpoint of faith.

These stages in his own development came to seem to Kierkegaard to be general stages in the development of human beings, who have the possibility of living at any of the stages permanently, or of moving from the lower to the higher. Each move to a higher stage must be something which the individual himself decides, for himself, to make. One cannot simply be told 'Adopt the standpoint of faith', nor could arguments, for instance the argument that one would be happier if one did, be sufficient to bring about the conversion. To be converted is to see for oneself that a certain belief or set of beliefs which one had previously held was false or inadequate. The new belief must be accepted, not merely as an intellectually preferable belief, nor merely as a belief based on satisfactory evidence, but as something which was true for the person who accepted it — that is as a truth by which he himself would be prepared to live, a truth, perhaps, which he loved.

It is from this feature of his work that it is possible to derive all that is most important and most characteristic in Existentialism, and in Existentialist ethics in particular. Kierkegaard wrote in order to free people from illusion. Now it might be argued that this is a somewhat trivial claim if properly examined, though it sounds grand enough. For, the argument would go, anyone who believes that what he says is true, and who, moreover, believes that he is the first to see this truth, or that other people have made mistakes — any such person writes in order to free his readers from illusion. If one even writes down the true proposition that today is Thursday, and does this in order to inform, then one does it also to free people from the possible illusion that today is Wednesday or Friday. To argue in this way would be to miss the peculiar point in the concept of illusion as employed by Kierkegaard; but it would also, I think typify a kind of response to Existentialist writing which is common and understandable enough.

To take the second point about response first: I should be inclined to regard it almost as a touchstone or criterion of an author's being classifiable as an Existentialist, that a reader may get impatient and accuse him of gross exaggeration and pretentiousness; that the reader may be inclined to deflate him and 'boil down' what he seems to be saying to some true but absolutely platitudinous remark. Thus, the impatient reader who is told that we face our freedom in anguish may say, 'All this amounts to is that often we are hard pressed to decide what to do'. So, faced with a claim that Kierkegaard wrote to free us from illusion, this same sceptic says, 'Well, so does the bank manager who writes to tell me I have an overdraft'. But in this case the word 'illusion' is the important one. It must be emphasised that an illusion is not a mere false belief, and that to replace illusion by true belief is to replace it by something, as I have already suggested, which is more than just the acceptance of an objectively true proposition. For to see something previously believed *as* illusion is to see it as to be detested; and to accept something as true is to accept it as illuminating to oneself *personally*. So, to live in a state of illusion is to live in a state in which one suffers from some total misconception, and to be freed from this condition is to see one's whole life in a totally new way. Kierkegaard would regard it as useless merely academically to put people right. He aimed to change them and set them on a different path.

The worst illusion, because the most persistent and most liable to dominate people's thought, and indeed to be welcomed by them, was, in his view, *objectivity*. We have lost the capacity for subjectivity and it is, he says, the task of philosophy to find this capacity for us. Objectivity may be characterised in various ways. It shows itself in the tendency to accept rules governing both behaviour and thought. Thus, any subject-matter which is bound by rules of evidence, or which can be properly taught in the class room, is in the grip of objectivity. History is objective if it is thought of as something in which the true can be definitely, once and for all, sifted out from the false, or if some absolute standard of what counts as good evidence or a conclusive argument is adopted. Morality is objective as soon as it is encapsulated in rules or principles which can be handed on from master to pupil or from father to son. The ethical phase of human development, as of Kierkegaard's own development, as we have seen, was characterised by the finding and observing of universal rules of conduct, held to be equally valid for everybody, and such that, in principle, they could have been written down.

He defines the objective tendency as that which 'proposes to make everyone an observer, and in its maximum to transform him into so objective an observer that he become almost a ghost, scarcely to be distinguished from the tremendous spirit of the historical past' and he says '. . . the ethical is, *becoming an observer!** That the individual must become an observer is the *ethical* answer to the problem of life . . .'.[1] To become an observer is to treat life as either history or as natural science. The historical standpoint raises the question 'What is my role in history?' or 'How will I look to future observers?' The scientific standpoint forces us perpetually to raise the question: 'By what natural law is human behaviour, including my own, determined?' Briefly, then, the objective is the rule-governed. It is the *myth* of objective truth which Kierkegaard above all wanted to explode. Hence was derived his hostility to science; for his *Concluding Unscientific Postscript* is in fact not so much unscientific as anti-scientific. But the sphere in which the myth of objectivity seemed to Kierkegaard not only dominating but also disastrous was religion — in particular, Christianity. For, though he returned to Christianity, it was not to the Christianity of his father. '. . . an objective acceptance of Christianity' he writes '(*sit venia verbo*) is paganism or thoughtlessness.' And '. . . Christianity protests against every form of objectivity; it desires that the subject should be infinitely concerned about himself. It is subjectivity that Christianity is concerned with, and it is only in subjectivity that its truth exists, if it exists at all; objectively, Christianity has absolutely no existence. If its truth happens to be only in a single subject, it exists in him alone; and there is greater Christian joy in heaven over this one individual than over universal history and the System . . .'[2]

It is the task of philosophy to convert people to the subjective. But subjectivity is extraordinarily difficult to achieve, for it is

* Present writer's italics.

apparently futile to strive to be what one already is, namely, an individual human being; and the tendency of all human beings is to fall into the trap of identifying themselves with something else, with some party or sect; or else, intellectually, to become impersonal, and to think of contributing to scientific knowledge absolutely. For the question of *whose* knowledge or *whose* truth it is becomes absurd, directly any newly-discovered proposition is added to the corpus of scientific knowledge in general. Therefore the individual may get lost, either in the acceptance of the dogma of a party or a creed, or in the acceptance of this body of scientific knowledge to which he may make contributions.

Subjective knowledge is different from objective knowledge in two ways. First, it cannot simply be passed on from one person to the next, nor added to by different researchers. There could be no such thing as the corpus of subjective knowledge. Secondly, what is known subjectively necessarily has the nature of a paradox, and must therefore require faith before it is known. Now faith is more like a sentiment than a thought, and everything that Kierkegaard says of subjective knowledge is appropriate rather to the emotions than to the intellect. Indeed he says: '. . . Christianity wishes to intensify passion to the highest pitch; but passion is subjectivity, and does not exist objectively.'

The absolute contrast between objective and subjective knowledge is brought out in the following passage: 'When the question of truth is raised in an objective manner, reflection is directed objectively to the truth, as an object to which the knower is related. Reflection is not focussed on the relationship, however, but upon the question whether it is the truth to which the knower is related. If only the object to which he is related is the truth, the subject is accounted to be in the truth. When the question of truth is raised subjectively, reflection is directed subjectively to the nature of the individual's relationship; if only the mode of this relationship is in the truth, the individual is in the truth even if he should happen to be thus related to what is not true.' And: 'When subjectivity, inwardness, is the truth, the truth becomes objectively a paradox; and the fact that the truth is objectively a paradox shows in its turn that subjectivity is the truth. For the objective situation (of entertaining a paradoxical thought) is repellent; and the expression for the objective repulsion constitutes the tension and the measure of the corresponding inwardness. The paradoxical character of the truth is its objective uncertainty; this uncertainty is the expression for the passionate inwardness and this passion is precisely the truth. . . . The eternal and essential truth, the truth which has an essential relationship to an existing individual because it pertains essentially to existence . . . is a paradox. But the eternal essential truth is by no means in itself a paradox; but it *becomes** paradoxical by virtue of its relationship to an existing individual.'3

The typical example of this tension between the objective uncertainty and the inward truth is that of the Socratic profession of ignorance, the claim to know nothing except that one knows nothing. The inwardness of Socrates was his whole life and method of philosophical enquiry, his asking of questions and shattering of accepted presuppositions and pretensions to knowledge. Objectively, the result of the Socratic enquiry was always to produce confusion and bewilderment. But, subjectively, it was the true method. So, analogously, in the true Christian, faith is the truth which is contrasted with the objective absurdity of his life. Socratic ignorance is the precursor of the *absurd*, and the Socratic life of seeking subjective truth is the precursor of the life of faith.

In these passages which I have quoted we have, it seems to me, the salient features of all subsequent Existentialist thought. This does not mean that all Existentialists deliberately derived all or any part of their thought from that of Kierkegaard; but rather that he first manifested the tendencies which are the mark of Existentialism, whoever practises it. First, there is the serious endeavour to remove from people the illusions by which they live — the illusions of objective moral law or objective scientific truth. There is such law and there is such truth, but both are essentially trivial and pointless, Secondly, the alternative to the illusion is the recognition that each person, in his own individual existence, must receive and understand a purely personal and

* Present writer's italics.

subjective truth. This truth cannot be stated in propositions which could be handed on to another person. Just as the individual has his own passions and his own life to live, so he has his own truth.

Most characteristically, then, Existentialism will undermine the distinction between thinking and feeling, between the rational and the sentimental. And, equally characteristically, it will preach a kind of doctrine which cannot be just accepted or rejected intellectually, but will essentially influence a person's life if he accepts it. So it is clear from considering this first example of Existentialist thought, i.e. the removal of illusion, that it would be absurd to expect a distinction between ethics and epistemology, between moral philosophy and the rest of philosophy. If there is any Existentialist ethics, it is to be extracted from this total view of the world, in which each man makes his own choice of the truth for himself. What we have here is not a system, for to create a system of philosophy was, in Kierkegaard's view, the very way to render philosophy pointless, something which could be thoughtlessly or merely academically read, and accepted or rejected as a whole. Each man must, we are told, *find* the truth in inwardness for himself. To objectify is to render truth trivial. For instance, to objectify religion leads to a watering-down of the central paradox. In the case of Christianity it leads to the attempt to rationalise and make easily acceptable the central paradox of the Incarnation.

Existentialism of this kind may be happily married to religion. And there have been other religious, or at least theistic, Existentialist thinkers, all of whom, to a greater or less extent, attempted descriptions of the personal and individual nature of the inward process which should lead a man to a true view of God and the universe. For example, I should at least mention the work of Gabriel Marcel, who was himself strongly influenced by Martin Büber in holding that the true essence or meaning of existence could be distilled in encounters between two persons, whether both human persons, or one human and one divine. It is easy to see how such a theory, since it explicitly seeks for a significance in the universe at large and finds it distilled in human life, might have a bearing on ethics, though not directly. For both how a man thinks he should behave, and how he thinks he should describe and analyse human behaviour as a whole, could be determined by a general view of the world in which human relationship of a personal kind was the highest value. In such a theory the essentially personal and individual nature of human experience is emphasised, even though this experience is thought to be *of* something other than mere human feelings and sensations, namely, *of* the transcendental. A man may freely choose to move to a stage of existence in which he can recognise and experience the transcendental in his own life; or, if he does not make the choice, his whole life may be given up to the illusion of the public, the agreed, the polite, and the scientific.

I want now to go on to suggest that, though this kind of belief is characteristically Existentialist, yet the foundation of such thought on a faith in God or the transcendental is by no means necessary to Existentialist philosophy; that the characteristic features of Existentialism are indeed intensified and made sharper if isolated in a purely human context. Once again I can hope to show this only by taking a single example, that of Heidegger.

III. HEIDEGGER

In the work of Martin Heidegger one can see the same features which emerged in Kierkegaard as characteristic of Existentialist thought. But it must be said that in more ways than one it is anomalous and perhaps unfair to class Heidegger as an Existentialist thinker at all. For one thing, as I have said already, he repudiates the description himself, and this ought to carry some weight; for another thing, there is one respect in which he comes at the opposite end of the philosophical scale from Kierkegaard. For he is above all an old-fashioned Hegelian system-builder, who aims to present the complete truth about the universe in absolute terms; and moreover his actual style of writing is pretentious, highflown, and dependent on technical jargon to an extent that would have disgusted Kierkegaard, the most hostile of all men to the pompous and self-important. Finally, although much of his description of human life seems, as we shall see, to be motivated by a Kierkegaardian desire to free his readers from illusion, and to explain how they may lead their lives in the truth, yet he himself denies any such motive, and claims that his terms of description are absolutely neutral and non-evaluative. I shall return to this later. For the moment it must be enough to say that on this point it seems impossible to take Heidegger at his word.

Despite these doubts, then, let us turn to Heidegger, or rather to those limited parts of his thought which have some relevance to the subject-matter of ethics. I shall not concern myself with the much-debated question whether Heidegger is really an atheist or not; I wish to concentrate on that part of his philosophy which is concerned with human beings and their existence in the world, and here, at least, there is no sign of theism to be found. It is here, too, that we can see a very natural development of Existentialist thought, for with the removal of any question of finding a relationship with God, or living according to some divine purpose, the scope of human freedom, the burdensomeness of choosing how to live, and of finding a system of values, is vastly increased. Heidegger tells us that there are two possible modes of existence, the 'authentic' and the 'inauthentic'. It is these terms which he claims, unplausibly, are entirely without evaluative connotation; they are, he says, simply descriptive of two ways of living. But if so, then he should have found some better words to describe them. And in fact the whole tenor of his thought, in so far as it is intelligible at all, is to present the inauthentic as something from which one can be helped by philosophy to escape. What, then, is this distinction? How does Heidegger make use of it?

Many of the ideas in Heidegger's description of human reality we shall look at again when they occur in the writings of Sartre; in Heidegger they are, in every case, more obscure, and it seems to me more ambiguous. I shall content myself here with the briefest possible summary.

Heidegger's main concern in *Sein und Zeit* (*Existence and Being*) is the problem of 'Being' in general. It is far from clear what this problem is, but at any rate the approach to its solution is said to be through the consideration of the nature of man, who stands in a peculiar relation to Being as a whole, because of his unique ability to raise questions about it. Man is the only being in the world who is capable of considering the nature of Being as a whole, and is therefore in a unique way exposed to it. Man is defined as 'potential existence'. This is to say that man is always *transcending* what he is at any given moment; he is always stretching towards the future and aiming at something which he is not yet. Furthermore, man is not a being in isolation. His existence is 'existence-in-the-world', and so he is conditioned, in every mode of his thought and action, not only by the material situation in which he finds himself but also, crucially, by other people in the world. Being bound up with other people is an essential mode of the existence of each of us. The being of man is 'being with' ('*mitsein*'). All individual or private concerns and standpoints exist only against the background of ways of thinking and looking common to men as members of a social group. The group is mankind at large, and is referred to as the 'One'. It is from the existence of the One as a necessary part of man's being that the distinction between authentic and inauthentic existence is derived. To accept one's role as a kind of generalised man, as *totally* part of the group, to be content with this, is to live inauthentically. It is possible, on the other hand, to seek to realise one's possibilities as an individual, alone, and as if one were isolated and independent. This is authentic existence. The way to achieve it is to treat one's life as a progress towards death, the only event, as Heidegger thinks, in which we are genuinely, each one of us, alone.

Sartre's exposition of Heidegger, in *Being and Nothingness*, is useful in helping us to understand the kind of failure involved in inauthenticity, and the kind of awakening which thinking about oneself in a new and philosophical way is intended to produce. He says: 'When I am in the inauthentic mode of the "they" the world offers me a sort of impersonal reflection of my possibilities, in the form of instruments and complexes of instruments which belong to "everybody", and which belong to me in so far as I am everybody: ready-made clothes, public transport, parks, gardens, common land, shelters made for *anyone* who needs them, and so on. . . . The inauthentic state, which is my ordinary state in so far as I have not realised my conversion to authenticity, reveals to me my "being with", not as the relation of one unique personality with another, not as the mutual connexion of "irre-placeable beings", but as a total interchangeability of the terms of the relation. I am not opposed to the other, for I am not "me"; instead, we have the social unity of the "they". . . . Authenticity and individuality have to be earned: I shall be my own authenticity only if, under the influence of the call of conscience, I launch out towards death, with resolution and decision, as towards my own particular possibility. At this moment I reveal myself to myself in authenticity, and I raise others along with myself towards the authentic.'[4]

There are several things to be noticed about the concept of authenticity as expounded. First of all, one may think that one has no choice but to launch oneself towards death, in any case.

After all, Heidegger is not advocating choosing death in a literal sense. Authenticity does not demand suicide. And if launching oneself towards death means living in the knowledge that one will die, then we all of us necessarily do this anyway. Further, it may be urged, it is a well-known absurdity to treat death as an event in one's life, still more as an event to be looked forward to as revealing oneself in some way. The whole elaborate apparatus of technical terms seems to do no more than remind us very obscurely that, for each of us, our life is our own, and we live only once.

dull, obvious remark, flatness.

I think there is justice in these remarks. We have noticed already that one common effect of the truly Existentialist writer is to provoke in his readers the exasperated desire to rewrite what he says in plain language, and to show that it doesn't after all amount to more than a platitude. If this is indeed a distinguishing mark of the Existentialist, then no one is so unambiguously an Existentialist as Heidegger. But a little more than the platitude that we are all mortal can be extracted from his philosophy.

For next, we may notice that the *call of conscience* leads us to question our own position in the ordinary pattern of social life. If we are to be what we are capable of being, we must not accept the given social situation, nor the ordinary ways of life involved in it, as the only or inevitable way. We must think of ourselves in a new relation to our background. Secondly, this new way of regarding ourselves amounts to treating ourselves as isolated, unique and free (and incidentally, though not much is made of this, we shall recognise that other people too are unique and free). This does not seem to entail, for Heidegger, any particular aims or goals, nor does it determine anything which would normally be called a morality. But the authentic life is the life, rather, in which, *whatever* we do, we are prepared to take full responsibility for it. We shall never be content to say 'It's what everyone does' or 'Society demands it'. Even if both these things are true, this will no longer constitute our *reason* for doing the things in question. Thus, presumably, if, even in the authentic state, I decide to take my children to the park, I decide to do so because this is something which I truly want to do, as a purposeful activity and as a fulfilment of some unique possibility of my own. I do not do it because I can't think of anything else to do with them, or because every one else does it. It seems impossible to make *precise* sense of the idea that my choices are all regarded, in the authentic state, as choices leading to my own private death; but perhaps the important imprecise point is that my choices are seen to be genuinely my own, and that I make them, knowing that I am free. I will never learn to see my deliberate actions in this way unless I contemplate the fact that there are some things, particularly dying, which happen to me individually and must be accepted and faced as happening to *me*.

What this amounts to more than anything, it seems to me, is a moral *tone of voice* of a recognisable kind. Existentialism largely consists in this tone. We have heard it in Kierkegaard, in a different context, and shall hear it again in Sartre. The suggestion is always that there is, if we will only face it, a deeper significance in what we do than we are ordinarily, in our unreflective state, prepared to allow. If we undergo the process of being freed from illusion, of being weaned from the ordinarily accepted categories and ways of judging things, then we see everything, and particularly our own life and actions, as meaning something, falling into place in a significant whole. It is for this reason that Existentialist writers characteristically have no separate ethical systems, but regard ethics as a part of a whole metaphysical or ontological scheme. For the deeper significance of our actions can emerge only if there is a wider whole for them to fit into.

Thus the whole plan of *Sein und Zeit*, incomplete though it is, is designed to put the existence of man in the context of the existence of everything, so that man can be seen to have a certain nature, in contrast with the modes in which everything else exists. This is metaphysical ethics, as practised, for instance, by Spinoza. But the upshot, in Heidegger's case, is perhaps the opposite of Spinozistic. We are supposed to see ourselves as really freer and more independent of the world than we imagined in our unregenerate state. And the conversion to authenticity can come about only if we are prepared to take ourselves enormously seriously, and devote ourselves to the cultivation of the subjective point of view. For most philosophers, especially empiricists, *subjectivity*, the fact that we see with our own eyes, feel our own pains, think our own thoughts, tends to constitute a problem. They have to account for the existence of a common and public world built out of these subjective and private elements. For Heidegger it is the opposite way round. We start with the common and public, and have to work our way towards the private and subjective. Only so will we become what we are capable of becoming, free responsible human beings.

ontological argument
- traditional argument for the existence of God: the concept necessitates existence

ontology - branch of metaphysics, nature of being

IV. J.-P. SARTRE

Turning to Jean-Paul Sartre, we are now in a position to trace those features of Existentialist thought which have appeared first in Kierkegaard and then, in a vast incoherent form, in Heidegger. In *Being and Nothingness*, Sartre's first large-scale philosophical work, we can see these features clearly, and make out their bearing on ethical philosophy. For Sartre, though not a particularly rigorous thinker, is at least a thoroughgoing one; and he has a gift for making memorable ideas which, though perhaps not original, become completely his own under his hand. It is for this reason that it has seemed convenient and perfectly proper to treat *Being and Nothingness* as the main source-book for Existentialist ethics. In this work, above all, we will catch the Existentialist tone.

Subjectivity, then, and *freedom* are the two main themes which we shall trace in *Being and Nothingness*. In his treatment of both themes the influence of Heidegger upon Sartre is very strong. I shall not, on the whole, attempt exact ascriptions of each thought or each item of philosophical terminology to an original. Not only would this be tedious but it would in a way also be misleading; for, as I have already said, Sartre makes ideas his own in a most idiosyncratic way.

SUBJECTIVITY

Sartre wrote: 'One cannot adopt the standpoint of the whole.' It is essential to his theory of the place of man in the universe (for *Being and Nothingness* attempts to expound nothing less than this) that any description of the world must be a description of the world as seen by somebody. Sartre takes over the Cartesian *cogito ergo sum* and uses it for his own purposes: he argues that our awareness of the world is always accompanied by a kind of vestigial awareness of ourselves, and that therefore consciousness of any kind is essentially a personal matter. I am conscious of the world *and* of myself — which amounts, together, to *my* world; you are conscious of the world and yourself — *your* world. The fundamental distinction upon which the whole structure of *Being and Nothingness* is based is the distinction between Beings-in-themselves and Beings-for-themselves, or conscious and self-conscious creatures. The 'Upsurge of Consciousness', which Sartre is prepared to mention as some far-distant historical occurrence, is by far the most important event that has ever happened in the universe. Beings-in-themselves, ordinary things, are essentially what they are. Rules can be given which govern their behaviour. This behaviour is invariable, and can in principle be predicted. In the case of *artefacts*, rules can be given laying down, with absolute accuracy, how they are to be made. General laws are relevant to Beings-in-themselves and can in principle be framed so as to exhaust their possibilities. None of this is true of Beings-for-themselves. These, *conscious beings*, are without essential natures.

Sartre is not here making a simple point about the uniqueness and idiosyncracy of human as opposed to other beings. The matter is rather more complicated. For he is not interested only in the common nature or essence of man, but even of *objects*, such as trees or ink-wells. Indeed, even when talking about material objects, he is sometimes almost obsessively concerned with the unique individuality of each. In *La Nausée*, for instance, Sartre's only philosophical novel, we have a long and powerful description of how the significance of the individual being of things was revealed to Roquentin, as he gazed fascinated at a tree-stump in the park.

This concentration on what it is to be a tree-stump or an ink-well or a glass, though put like that may sound absurd, has its historical origin in the *epoche* which the German phenomenologists, Brentano, Meinong, and Husserl, demanded. They required that a philosopher should concentrate on the content of his consciousness, including his objects of perception, in themselves, as they appeared to him, when he had laid aside all the normal presuppositions, expectations, and labels with which, in our non-philosophical moments, we are equipped. The influence of Husserl is particularly strong on Sartre in all his early writings, and it is perhaps the mixture of phenomenology with the sources of Existentialism we have already looked at which makes Sartre's own version of Existentialism so much the most rewarding to philosophers. But this is by the way. In Sartre's hands the doctrines of phenomenology amount to this, that we must try to think of things without their names and their ordinary descriptions, but in their essence as they actually appear to us. And we shall find that, although the things we observe may, as it were, overflow the verbal containers we put them in, though they may, to a certain extent, escape through the net of our concepts and our language, yet, up to a point, they are amenable to being labelled, they do abide by the rules which we make for them, in the form of scientific laws, they do have shared essences, even though each thing is also an individual.

This is so simply because material objects are without *aspirations*. They cannot try, or hope, or wish, or long to be other than they are. And it is for this reason that they are said to be what they are *completely*. They are solid (*massif*). Consciousness, on the other hand, consists in the power to be aware not only how things *are*, but how they are *not*. The possibility of conceiving a situation negatively, either as *not* what it was, or as *not* what one would like, or as *not* what one could make it, is of the utmost importance in Sartre's account of human consciousness, and thus of the human position in the world as a whole. Consciousness is said to be a gap or space between the conscious being and the world. I think it is possible to see what Sartre means by this. By thinking about something, or barely being aware of it, one distinguishes between this something and one's self. As we have seen, he thinks that in perceiving something, if one is fully conscious of the object, one is also at least minimally conscious of oneself, though this self-consciousness may be more or less acute or reflective. This self-awareness in perception entails the drawing of a distinction between the observer and the object of observation, and to draw such a distinction is thought of as separating the observer and the thing observed by a space. This space, or gap, which is created by putting the world at a distance from oneself, is the essential characteristic consciousness, and is sometimes referred to by Sartre as an emptiness or nothingness within the observer himself.

It is through the existence of this emptiness, separating a person from the world of things about him, that the possibility arises of thinking or acting as one chooses. There is necessarily, in a conscious being, an area of free play, as it were, between himself and the world. The emptiness within him has to be filled, and is filled by whatever he plans to do, or to think, or to be. Consciousness, Sartre says, knowingly places itself at a distance from its objects, and the gap between itself and its objects is identical with the power to confirm or deny what it chooses. Freedom and consciousness thus turns out to be the very same thing. They are both identified with the power to consider things either as they are or as they are not, to imagine situations which are different from the actual situations obtaining in the world; and therefore to form plans to change what there is.

It is impossible to exaggerate the importance of the power to conceive negatively in Sartre's systematic account of the world. There is no bridging the gulf between conscious beings and unconscious beings. They are divided by this vast difference, the difference between being able and not being able to conceive of *what is not the case*. Though Sartre does not examine this aspect of his thesis in detail, it would be plausible to maintain that the difference he is insisting on is really that between language-users and non-language-users. For the possibility of description, in language, does depend on the realisation that each item of experience should be described so and *not otherwise*; that is, if an object is black, it follows that it is not-white, that 'not-white' is an alternative, though vaguer, description of it. To be able to describe, notoriously, one must be able to describe truly *or falsely*. There would in fact be something to be said for making Sartre's distinction in this way, partly because he is himself very much interested in the fact that we freely choose the descriptions, and even the basic categories, under which we classify our world;

partly because animals could, in this scheme, be separated from men, without thereby having to be classified as unconscious beings. Sartre is prepared, I believe, to classify animals as unconscious; but this makes one suspect uneasily that his notion of consciousness must be a bit different from the normal use. However, this is not a problem that should detain us here.

The fundamental relation, then, between conscious beings and the world is derived by Sartre from the power of negation. Thinking of how things are *not* is the indispensable preliminary to describing them, categorising them, seeing them as desirable or hateful, and therefore to trying to change them. We can sum up this fundamental relation under the technical term 'projection'. Human projects upon the world include perception of it, knowing it, feeling things about it, making plans to change it, and intervening in its course. We have seen, furthermore, that this power of negation, which marks off the conscious from the unconscious items in the world, is connected by very strong links with freedom, and indeed can be identified with freedom. Freedom can be identified, that is, with the ability to see things as possibly other than they are, or with human imagination. I shall have more to say about freedom itself in the next section. But for the moment let us notice that this connection between freedom and negation makes it inevitable that, in *Being and Nothingness*, Sartre should concentrate so strongly in the individual. This is only to say that in this part of his philosophical writing, he provides metaphysical backing of the most general possible kind for his Existentialist concern with the world and free action seen from the point of view of one man. For in describing human consciousness, and placing it in its metaphysical context in the world, he is necessarily concerned with human action.

It is impossible to act without a motive, to act, that is, as opposed to merely letting something happen to one. To have a motive is to conceive a project for the future, which in turn entails, as we have seen, the power to conceive the future negatively, as filled with situations and states of affairs not yet in being. Consciousness, that is to say, is necessarily consciousness of the world from the point of view of a potential *agent*. My acts are necessarily my own, if I am free; and I cannot be properly conscious of the world, or know or say anything about it at all, without thereby being prepared to act on the world. There is no such thing as bare consciousness unconnected with action. A state of affairs cannot in itself be a motive for action; only the awareness of a state of affairs as something to be changed can be. For instance, if I am very cold, it might be thought that the cold was my motive for getting up and putting more coal on the fire. But the cold itself cannot, according to Sartre, lead me to *act* at all. It can merely lead to a passive experiencing of it, or acceptance of it. What constitutes my motive for getting up for the coal, is my apprehension of the cold *as something to be overcome*, as something intolerable, which need not persist into the imagined future. I regard it, in Sartre's jargon, as *dépassable*. He gives many illustrations from history to show the difference between being truly aware of one's situation as unbearable and as something which could be changed, and being merely passively half-aware of it, enduring it without the belief that it is only a stage, from which one could move on to a better stage. The possibility of revolution depends, in this early doctrine, entirely upon the possibility of the individual worker being able to envisage a future for himself personally which does not resemble his past, and therefore being able freely to choose or project a change. So, free action stems from the gap which constitutes consciousness and which separates a man from the world in which he is, enabling him to imagine and envisage what is not the case.

The concept of 'projection' is, as we have seen, of extremely wide extension. Perceiving, knowing, feeling, planning, and acting are all embraced in it. There is therefore, for Sartre, no radical distinction to be drawn between all these things. This grouping together of things usually thought of as distinct has important consequences for ethical theory. For one thing, Sartre's concept of feeling or of the emotions, which is manifestly relevant to ethics, is determined by his treatment of emotions as 'on all fours' with other kinds of 'projects' upon the world. It is worth examining this treatment, however briefly, since it is impossible to understand the nature of Sartre's subjectivist approach to ethical theory without fully understanding this relation of 'projection', especially as it applies to the emotions. (In this part of his theory, once again, he is strongly influenced by Husserl and phenomenology.)

Roughly speaking, his thesis is that emotions, like other states of consciousness, are intensional, that is, they are directed upon an object. They are also modes of apprehension. That is to say, if I am angry, I am angry *about* something, and it is this that is meant by the intensionality of the emotion; my anger is my *way* of being aware of what I am angry about. But not only so: my being aware of the object of my anger in this particular way is a part of my purposes. When I behave angrily, I mean something, I have an end in view. Emotions in general all mean something. They are purposive in the same sort of way as words are. We aim always, according to Sartre, to reduce our world to order, to manage it for our own ends, to control it for our particular purposes. But sometimes the world is recalcitrant, and will not be managed as we should like. It is then that we have recourse to emotional responses, when other responses and other modes of apprehension break down or are ineffective.

He illustrates this by the case of a girl who goes to see her doctor, rationally intending to make some confession to him which she does not really want to make. She *therefore*, according to Sartre, breaks down in tears, in order that it shall be impossible for her to speak. When we have recourse to emotion we are pretending to ourselves that we can get what we want by a kind of magic. We lapse into an infantile view of the world in which things happen which we know rationally cannot happen. The girl at the doctor's knows that she cannot really make it impossible for herself to speak by crying; but she is pretending that this can happen.

All our perceptions of the world, as we have seen, relate to our own purposes. We see the world essentially as a place to do things in. But sometimes things are too disagreeable or too difficult to be managed. The world is seen as making impossible demands on us. When this happens we cannot face taking ordinary scientifically accredited steps to achieve our ends, not can we bear to admit that we cannot achieve them. And so it is that we pretend we can get what we want by non-scientific means. The power to lapse into the magical way of apprehending things is connected by Sartre with the power of imagination, and is one of the great powers that conscious beings have, all of them derived from the negating power of consciousness. This magical mode of apprehension *is* emotion. Sartre says: 'Emotion is a transformation of the world. When the paths before us become too difficult, or when we cannot see our way, we no longer put up with so exacting a world. All ways are barred, and yet we must act. So then we try to change the world; that is, to live it as though the relation between things were not governed by deterministic processes, but by magic.'[5] We *try to change the world*: there is, thus, no essential difference between feeling and acting. Feeling, or the experience of emotions, is, in Sartre's view, a kind of futile and frustrated action. He illustrates this first by the somewhat frivolous example of a man who sees some grapes which he wants, but finds he cannot reach them. So he pretends to himself that they were too sour anyway, and so feels disgust at the thought of eating them. He cannot turn them into sour grapes by chemistry, but he changes them to sour grapes by magic so that he can feel positive relief at not having to eat them. Sartre admits that this little drama played out under the vine does not amount to much. But, he says, let the situation become one of life or death, and there we have emotion. If we are terrified, we cannot get rid of the object of our fear by rational or scientific means, so in extreme cases we may even faint, to blot out the terrifying world, or we may try to eliminate it by running away. Sometimes, when we are in a generally emotional condition, we may see the world as already magical, and then we see everything in the world with an emotional colour. For instance, if we are happy, we may feel that everything is within our power, and this is a magical, not a true, power. Again, if we are frightened suddenly, then we may fear things which scientifically speaking could do us no harm (such as a spider, or the expression of someone's face) because we have relapsed from believing in ordinary cause and effect into a primitive condition of believing in magic. For the time being the world, which in fact remains the same for everyone else, is transformed for the individual into something different, and it is for his own purposes that he so transforms it. Though we may feel as if we are *overcome* by emotion and that it has nothing to do with what we want or plan, this is an illusion, according to Sartre, from which we would do well to free ourselves. What we feel depends on what we personally plan to do. Indeed, it is a part of our general design upon the world. If we changed our plan, and with it our way of looking at the world, we would change our feelings too. We cannot explain emotion, or fit it into the general picture of the world, without explaining how the particular individual who experiences the emotion sees his world.

The theory of the emotions illustrates the main theme of *Being and Nothingness*. Whatever mode of consciousness we consider, it will be explicable only if it is viewed as a project for an individual, the plan or purpose of a particular human being. And thus it is that the difference between knowing, doing, and feeling is ironed out. But it must be said that there is a great objection to accepting any such view, and this objection is felt as strongly in reading Sartre as in reading Kierkegaard or Heidegger. It is in fact repugnant not only to common sense but to all rationality, to refuse to distinguish between knowing and doing. The difference is in fact ineradicable. Knowledge is, in an important sense, impersonal. If something is true, then it can be known, no matter by whom. My knowledge, if properly so called, can be thought of as literally identical with your knowledge. Whereas of my actions I, and I alone, am the author. Choice, we might admit, must be the choice of one person alone; but knowledge, if it deserves the name, must in principle be sharable.

The consequence of the grouping of all human projects together in this way is, then, to concentrate attention primarily on the individual and his personal assessment of and dealings with the world. And this general point of view necessarily determines what kind of ethical system could be derived from Sartre's philosophy. It will not surprise us to learn that Sartre thought each one of us had to devise his *own* morality, and make his *own* choices without the help of rules or principles. We shall return again and again to this point.

It must be noticed, however, that in spite of this concentration on the individual, Sartre rejected any kind of solipsism as non-sensical. For part of the self-awareness which each of us has, along with our awareness of the world, is derived from our awareness of others. Not only could we not be aware of the world without being aware of other people in it, but in an important way we could not be aware of ourselves. Other people bring us into real existence, or rather, they complete the existence we have. Being-for-others is another and essential aspect of the existence of every Being-for-itself. For instance, it is other people who make us see how what we are doing is to be described. They make us think of possible categories for our actions, and so we ascribe these actions to ourselves and feel pride or shame in them. Other people, as it were, attach labels to us; they say we are stupid, clever, dishonest, cautious, and so on; and in the light of these labels we live our lives. We are propped up on all sides by the view which other people have of us; sometimes it is a help and sometimes a hindrance, but without it we should not be fully aware of ourselves in the world.

Sartre gives an example of a man who, out of jealousy or malice, listens at a keyhole. He supposes himself to be unobserved, and he is completely absorbed in what he hears. In a sense he is only just aware of *himself* at all. He is nothing except what he does. But then he hears footsteps behind him and he realises that someone is watching him. At this moment, Sartre says, he comes into existence again as a person distinct from his actions. He is someone who is doing deliberately something of which he is ashamed. It is essential that he should relate his action to himself as a person in order to feel shame; and this possibility was brought about for him just at the moment when he heard the footsteps.

Besides cases like this, in which awareness of the look of the other is constitutive of our knowledge of ourselves, there are other ways in which the existence of other people modifies our description of our own act, or at least seems to render it dubious and incomplete. For there is a constant possibility of conflict between our own view of ourselves and other people's view of us. It would often be a matter of extreme complexity, and would perhaps require a novelist or a playwright, to work out the details of this kind of conflict in a given case. But that there might here be a profitable subject for investigation by moral philosophers is obviously true.

Here, it seems, is an area, one of many, in which Existentialist moral philosophy is richer and more subtle, at least potentially, than other systems of ethics, which tend to assume one uniform objective standpoint. The realisation that other people regard one, let us say, as predictably unpunctual, whereas from one's own point of view each instance of unpunctuality is just a matter of chance, just bad luck, and nothing to do with one's character (there is no reason to think one will not be in time on the next occasion), the realisation that for others, perhaps, one's promises are worthless, and one's resolutions unreal, is shocking and unacceptable. It inevitably raises questions about what is the *proper* description of one's conduct. In any account of ethics, particularly an account which includes discussion of the concept of character, or of virtues and vices, it would be an over-simplification if the possibility of this double vision of one and the same situation were left out. In short, the part which other people's view of us plays in our lives is something in which Existentialist philosophers are right to interest themselves.

Consciousness of being looked at by other people, of being an object of attention or of assessment for them, is a fundamental part of our awareness of the world and of ourselves, and therefore solipsism is a theory which it is in fact impossible to adopt, and contradictory to formulate. We feel the presence of others, Sartre says, and it touches us to the heart. We could no more deny it than we could deny our own existence. I shall return later to the question which naturally follows from this, namely, 'What is our relationship with other people in the world', or 'What ought it to be?' For the moment it is enough to suggest that the existence of others is structurally a part of our world, on the Existentialist view, and that *their view of us* will have to be taken into account in moral theory, as well as our view of them.

We have seen that according to Sartre's theory consciousness and freedom are in essence the same. If we are conscious beings, in his sense, then we are also free. We fill our lives by freely choosing not only what to *do*, but also what to feel and think, what to believe, and how to describe things. We may choose to see things as frightening or beautiful, disgusting or attractive, and from this kind of choice springs our character, our attitudes, and our way of life. Each one of us, naturally, has to make these choices for himself. As his consciousness is his alone, so are his choices. We must now consider what are the consequences for the possibility of ethical theory of this vast, unbounded freedom. Sartre says: 'Our point of departure is in fact the subjectivity of the individual, and this for strictly philosophical reasons . . . because we want a doctrine based on the truth.'[6] This truth is the truth revealed by the *cogito* of Descartes' 'I think'. The *cogito* reveals to us both that we are conscious, and that we can think of the world as waiting to be changed by us. We discover in it our own emptiness; we find that we are nothing but what we do and think. A man is nothing but his life, and he can fill his life as he chooses. There are two principal relations in which a man manifests his freedom to choose. The first is his relation with himself, in which he may choose to cast himself in a certain role in life; the second is his relations with other people.

BAD FAITH

The first important truth about a man's freedom is that it is unbearable. Seriously to face the world, as Sartre thinks that we should, knowing that everything is open to us, that we may do or be anything that we choose, is something which most of us would find hard to put up with; for what has been removed from us is the comfort of excuses. We are no longer, if Sartre is right, in a position to say 'I couldn't help' doing this or that. We may no longer even say 'I can't help feeling' this or that. We *can* help it, and if we do anything or become anything it is fundamentally not because we have to, but because we want to. This is a harsh thought, and in the face of it we suffer anguish. It is the agony of knowing that everything is up to us. There is no one on whom to shuffle off responsibility. Sartre identifies this anguish with what Kierkegaard described as the 'anguish of Abraham'. When Abraham hears the voice of the angel telling him to sacrifice his son Isaac, he obeys; but he may realise afterwards that it was in fact his choice to *take* the voice to be a genuine message from God. There could never be any proof that it was genuine. Therefore, believing that the voice was the voice of the angel was his own act, and thus sacrificing his son in obedience to it was his own act too. No one but he was responsible.

However, most of us do not experience this anguish, at any rate not all the time. This is because we cannot bear to; and we devise ways of escaping it, by concealing our freedom from ourselves. The most common way that we do this is by lapsing into 'Bad Faith'. Bad Faith consists in pretending that we are not free, that we are somehow determined, that we cannot help doing what we do, or having the role that we have. A description of the various kinds of pretences that we adopt, and an account of the origin of our ability so to pretend, occupies a large part of *Being and Nothingness*. As we should expect, the very possibility of Bad Faith derives from the nature of human consciousness, and therefore it is shown that if one were not in fact free one could not adopt the pretence that one was not. For Bad Faith, like the rest of our conscious apprehension of the world, depends on the power to stand back and distinguish ourselves from our surroundings. To be able to pretend means to be able to see things as otherwise than they are. I cannot pretend to be a bear unless I know that I am not a bear and yet deliberately adopt behaviour which I conceive to be suitable for bears. It is, of course, possible to pretend to be oneself, or oneself in a certain aspect. This is, once again, to stand back and see oneself in a certain role and then play the role as hard as one can. Very small children are capable of this: they may start by saying to their mother, 'You be the little girl and I'll be the mother'. But then they often move on to say, 'Now you be the mother, and I'll be the little girl', and they then go through, as it were at one remove, and rather quickly, all the things they usually do, such as having lunch and going to bed. In this situation they are *seeing themselves as* 'the little girl', instead of just being such. Playing at being what one in fact is can become a way of seeming to oneself to be determined, to have no choice but to do whatever 'little girls' *do*.

This deliberate filling of a role, so that one may seem to one-self to have no choices left — one's actions to be totally determined by the role — this is one of the two typical kinds of Bad Faith. Sartre illustrates it by the brilliant description of the waiter in the café.[7] All his movements and gestures are a little overdone, Sartre says. His behaviour seems ritualistic, like part of a game. The game he is playing is the game of 'being a waiter'. All tradesmen, all public figures have an expected, ritualistic manner; they have their own peculiar 'dance'. The outside world expects them to behave in this way, and indeed is worried if they move outside the proper steps and turns. 'A grocer who dreams is offensive to the buyer, because such a grocer is not wholly a grocer.' To be *wholly* whatever it is, a waiter, a grocer, a judge, is the aim, too, of the man himself who is acting the part. All conscious beings, beings-for-themselves, are without essence, as we have seen. They have to choose their life, and so choose what they are. Beings-in-themselves, on the other hand, are *massif*. They are wholly and unambiguously, for ever, what they are. Conscious beings long for this safe, solid condition. The hollow-ness which afflicts them is the same as their freedom, and it is burdensome. So the aim of Bad Faith is to bring a man as near as possible to the condition of a thing, an object, to be simply summed up in a word, a *pure* waiter through and through, who has no more choice of how to behave than a robot-waiter has. From within, Sartre says, the waiter sees himself as a person with duties, rights, conditions of employment, and so on. But to see oneself as this is to stand back and see something abstract: '. . . it is precisely this person *who I have to be* . . . and who I am not. . . . I am separated from him as the object from the subject, separated *by nothing*, but this nothing isolates me from him. I cannot be he,

31

I can only play at *being* him. . . . What I attempt to realise is a being-in-itself of the café waiter.'[7] To make this attempt is to conceal from myself that it is in fact I, and I alone, who confer value and urgency on the things which I say I *must* do, which I say are *part of the job*, which I feel *bound* to do. I get up at five, I get the coffee ready, saying that I have to; but in fact I *need* not. I could choose to stay in bed late, and be sacked. I could fail to prepare coffee, or pour it down the neck of the first customer. That I do not do these things is not because I cannot or must not. It is because I do not *choose* to. The realisation that it is I who confer values and who make rules for myself is like the realisation of Abraham that it was *he* who decided that he must obey the voice. In playing out his role, the waiter is seeking to avoid the anguish of Abraham.

→ Another mode of Bad Faith is that in which we may pretend that we are thing-like in the sense of being just a body, just another object in the world, which we can observe having things happen to it which are in a way nothing to do with us. The same detachment from ourselves, the treating of ourselves as an object of observation, is characteristic of this kind of Bad Faith as well. Once again Sartre illustrates this in a marvellous little story of a girl who is taken out by a man, and who, in order to preserve the particular excitement of the occasion, and to put off the realisation that there are decisions to be made, pretends not to notice his intentions, and who finally gets involved in intellectual conversation and leaves her hand to be taken by him, as if it were nothing to do with her.[8] The hand just rests in his, inert and thing-like. If she had removed it or deliberately left it where it was, she would in either case have faced the facts and made a definite decision. But by simply not taking responsibility for her hand and what is happening to it, she has evaded the need to decide, for the time being. This is Bad Faith.

In considering these examples — and they could be endlessly multiplied — we may feel inclined to raise the question of the relevance of Bad Faith to morality. Admittedly we can recognise the kind of self-deception and posing involved in Bad Faith, but is it so very bad? Has the waiter done anything *wrong* in playing his part as he does, even if at times he has slightly over-played it? The worst we could say of him, it seems, is that he is a bit absurd; or that he has an air of unreality about him. In answer to this, I think that Sartre would say the waiter was wrong — not *harmful* perhaps, but wrong. And here we may see emerging an absolutely essential feature of Existentialist ethics. Pretence, pretentiousness, wilful ignorance, blind adherence to convention, all these are wrong, because they are obstacles to free choice. This view is common to Kierkegaard and Sartre and, less clearly, to Heidegger (can he really be hostile to pretentiousness?) and to all Existentialists. It is a view of extraordinary severity. Sartre would doubtless agree that often good, in the sense of good results, might derive from someone's seeing himself as some character, and acting the part well. Good might come from a judge, a soldier, a policeman, indeed from any tradesman or professional man, successfully sustaining the role of a devoted and conscientious member of his trade or profession. And nearly always, as he says, there is a public demand that this should happen. But the good that might come from it would be entirely irrelevant to the moral worth of the man.

I do not mean I suggest that either Kierkegaard or Sartre would use such explicitly Kantian a term as 'moral worth' to express this thought. But I think there is something Kantian in the particular ruthlessness of judgment which is involved. Kant was prepared to admire or to like a virtuous disposition in a man, which produced agreeable or useful results. But he did not think that this kind of good was in any way relevant to the *moral* goodness or *moral worth* of a man. Goodness of the moral kind was to be had only in choosing to act in accordance with the categorical moral imperative. For Sartre, of course, there was no categorical moral imperative. So far from thinking that choosing according to rules of absolute duty would give moral worth to a man, he thought it nothing but Bad Faith to pretend that there were such rules. In this way his conclusion might seem to be the very opposite of Kant's. But the important point of resemblance is simply this, that for both of them, unless a decision to do something is a free choice, made in the knowledge and conviction that it is a free choice, then it is absolutely impossible that it should have any moral value.

The difference between them lies in what counts for each as free choice. Rational decision in accordance with the principle of the categorical imperative, the great rule which rational agents impose upon themselves, for no other end than that it is rational — this is the only free decision, according to Kant. For only reason is free. Man in his non-rational aspects is just another object in the world, as animals and trees, though living, are just objects, and subject to deterministic laws of nature. Thus, acting according to inclination or instinct or habit is not free voluntary action at all. It is just letting things happen. There is one and only one way to break out of the deterministic pattern of events, and that is by following another law than the law of nature, namely, the autonomous law of reason. The form which this law of reason took, for Kant, was that we should act only on such a principle as we could rationally envisage as universal. That is, whatever we choose for ourselves must be what we would also choose for others. It is impossible *rationally* to choose to make an exception for oneself. Now we shall see in a moment that there was a time when Sartre toyed with an almost purely Kantian account of what constituted free choice. But no such Kantian adherence to the law of reason, whatever this may be, is actually implied in the concept of Bad Faith itself, nor in the injunction to avoid it. Indeed, in *Being and Nothingness*, there is considerable lack of clarity about what a perfectly and genuinely free choice would be. We have the uneasy feeling that whatever choice we make there must come a time when we might say: 'Very well, I *must* do this', but that if we went on to give reasons why it must be done, we should be told that it *need not* be done, and we should be accused of Bad Faith. It looks as if there is never any possible proof that we are not guilty of Bad Faith.

What will be admitted as the real limit to our freedom? Surely there must be some things that we *cannot* do, and some circumstances where quite genuinely, and without self-deception, we can say 'I had no choice'? It sometimes looks as if Sartre would never in any circumstances allow the excuse 'I couldn't do anything except . . .'. If Bad Faith is so absolutely universal and ubiquitous as he sometimes suggests, then not only do we feel that it cannot be so very wrong but it also ceases to be of much interest as a moral category. To point to the universal human predicament is not enough, as the foundation for ethics.

→ But, for what it is worth, I do not think that the category of Bad Faith is a wholly useless or uninteresting category. It is just that, as we have seen earlier, Existentialism of every kind is prone to exaggeration. Not only Sartre, but Kierkegaard, Heidegger, Büber, and others are liable to have a fruitful and illuminating central idea and overwork it. Sartre, for instance, is in danger of rendering futile both the concept of choice and that of freedom itself by supposing them applicable everywhere. But if we avoid exaggeration, then we may see that there are indeed kinds of characters in describing which no concept is more useful than that of Bad Faith; and that in the case of such people a full moral description, including an assessment of their moral responsibility for their actions, could not be given without recourse to such a concept.

The kind of character I have in mind is that of whom it would be impossible to answer simply whether they were sincere or insincere, whether their professions of enthusiasm or interest, for example, were genuine or derived from some picture of themselves which, for the time being, they were making real. Sometimes it may be very important to come to a conclusion on this kind of question. Can we rely on consistency in their views, or not? Is another picture of themselves likely to be superimposed on the existing one, to bring with it a whole lot of new tastes and interests, or not? There is a whole range of human judgments, not only of reliability or otherwise, but of niceness and nastiness, trustworthiness, and so on, which depend on the question, 'Does he mean what he says?' But even if the answer to this is yes, there may still be further questions: 'Why does he hold this view? Will he always hold it? Can we imagine his holding a different one?' Sometimes, in the case of a person about whom this question of sincerity seems urgently in need of an answer, it would be going too far to say of him that he was positively insincere. But it would be right to say that he acted often, or usually, in Bad Faith. He may, let us say, see himself at different times in different roles. And the role of the moment will determine his behaviour, dictate his views, regulate how much money he spends, control his attitude to sex, social class, sport, everything.

It does not matter whether the role is that of a professional man of some sort, or, more insidiously, that of a member of some admired social group. It may be that living in a certain part of London, for instance, may make a man think of himself as a certain kind of person. And then, though he will not consciously alter his tastes and habits, yet some kinds of behaviour, some kinds of furniture or books or modes of speech, may come to seem impossible, and some kinds of expenditure, for instance on food and drink or a particular kind of holiday, may seem absolutely necessary. This is Bad Faith. It is not vicious; and it is not insincere. The man who suddenly becomes interested in a fashionable subject, or who finds that all his friends have titles, does indeed become interested, does truly like the people with the titles. It is just that he does so, perhaps, because he has decided to adopt the role of that kind of person — a modern intellectual, a well-connected man. The trouble with Bad Faith is that it leads to a gulf between a man's way of looking at himself and other people's way of looking at him, a gulf which we have noticed before. The intellectual of fashionable tastes will think of himself as having this genuine interest. To others he will seem to be jumping onto some profitable band-wagon. The man whose friends are dukes will seem to himself to like the dukes despite their titles. To others he will seem a snob. And the wider the gulf is between our view of ourselves and other people's view of us, the more we are in danger of losing our identity. If for others I am just a snob, all my actions and tastes predictable, then even to myself my allegedly free choice of friends is likely to begin to look a bit unreal. The man who has a part and slightly overplays it, like Sartre's waiter, has an air of unreality and staginess about him. In contrast with this, the alternative, actually to form projects and to put them into practice freely, knowing that one is free, and clear-sightedly to do what one wants in each situation, seems both admirable and attractive.

So far, then, the man who is excessively guilty of Bad Faith has emerged as an unadmirable and unattractive man, living a life of fantasy, acting out the role of the businessman, the good fellow, the scholar, whatever it may be. But there is also a use of Bad Faith which has an even closer bearing on morals. One of the manifestations of Bad Faith to which Sartre constantly calls attention is the habit we may fall into of thinking of our lives as a path along which duties lie in wait for us, waiting to be fulfilled. We may tend to think that some things are required of us, and that if we do these we shall have done all we can or need do; that if we go about armed with a list of duties, and keep our eyes open for reasonable chances to fulfil them, then we shall be leading satisfactory moral lives. This habit, which is very natural, is reinforced by the teaching of moral philosophers who try to show either that there are some absolute duties, in the fulfilling of which, for their own sake, moral worth consists; or that no moral act can ever be performed which is not performed in the belief that such an act in such a situation would *always* be the proper thing to do, for everyone. The doctrine that such an attitude to morality is Bad Faith has an enormous significance for ethics. For it suggests that, instead of coming to situations armed with lists or sets of principles, some one of which has got to be put into practice, we must think of each situation afresh, and try to see what, stock descriptions, duties and principles apart, ought to be done for the best. If we are faced with a situation in which we have to make a moral decision, on this view, we must really decide *for ourselves*, what to do remembering that we *could* decide anything, and not seeking to evade responsibility by sheltering under the rules, the principles, what one *must* do in such a case. It is possible that our decision may be the same in outcome as what we would have decided with the help of a handbook of duties and forbidden acts. But sometimes it may not. And whichever way it is, our decision will have the merit of having been reached after thought about what exactly the situation is, and what the case in question really involves. Knowing what we are up to in deciding to do this or to do that, seeing clearly who we are and what exactly we are doing, this is the ideal which is approachable through the avoidance of Bad Faith.

OTHER PEOPLE

It is now time to return to what is perhaps the most important question of all, namely how, in Sartre's view, we should take account of other people in our moral life. For ethics must be defined as the theory of how people should live *together*. Moreover, as we have seen, for Sartre the existence of others is, metaphysically speaking, a constitutive part of the life of each one, and thus *a fortiori* must be part of his moral life. Also, it would be generally agreed that the desires and wishes of others, their interests and their liberty, constitute a limit to the morally desirable exercise of our own freedom to satisfy *our* desires. This moral platitude, which, though platitudinous, is the very foundation of morality, must have particular importance for the Existentialists, who preach the doctrine of absolute and total human freedom. For them, if freedom and its exercise are the highest good, the problem of the distribution of freedom, the reconciling of my freedom with yours, must, one might argue, present the greatest problem of all. Their systems of ethics should consist largely in its solution.

But here we come upon a paradox. For though it seems obvious that some solution to this problem must be the beginning of any ethical theory for the Existentialists, in fact they are curiously silent on the subject. Or, if it is not fair to say that they are silent, perhaps we should say that they are inconclusive. It is here that the influence of Hegel perhaps makes itself most, and most unhappily, felt. We have seen already that Heidegger's ethical theory was primarily designed to show the supreme value of Authentic life; and this meant the Authentic facing of death by each man. Other people come into this picture of life only as part of the scenery, part of that human situation which each one of us has voluntarily to accept. There is a sort of heroism in this attitude, but very little humanity. Hegel regarded the reconciling of diverse human interests as mainly a matter for law; at a metaphysical level he regarded human relations as necessarily consisting in conflict. In Heidegger too there is the same failure on, as Sartre would say, the best philosophical grounds, to take other people's interests seriously. And in *Being and Nothingness* this failure seems to me to lead in the end to the collapse of any attempt at a satisfactory ethical theory. But before I attempt to show how this comes about, we should first look at an approach to the solution of the problem which Sartre at one time tried, and which, though he afterwards repudiated it, nevertheless gained a good deal of publicity. I am referring to the essay entitled *Existentialism and Humanism* which was published in 1946.[6] This essay has been translated several times into English, and when English readers were first becoming interested in the writings of Sartre this was one of the first things they read. Furthermore, A. J. Ayer, and several other philosophers, referred to it as containing a clear statement of Sartre's ethical position. However, it seems that Sartre himself regretted its publication. The specifically ethical views in it are different from any that could be derived from *Being and Nothingness*, and at one point, as we shall see, they were later directly contradicted by Sartre himself. So, though it is necessary to look at the essay for the sake of historical completeness, and perhaps to see it as containing a possible doctrine for an Existentialist thinker to hold, yet it would be misleading to treat it as properly the theory of Sartre himself.

The main burden of this essay is that, contrary to popular opinion, existentialism is a basically optimistic philosophy. For, Sartre says, it encourages men to action by teaching them that their destiny is in their own hands, and that there is no possibility of living except by acting. There is no despair, he suggests, in a theory according to which we have to decide for ourselves how to live, and we create ourselves, become whatever we are, by making decisions. So far there is nothing here which could not have come from *Being and Nothingness*. But the peculiarity of the essay becomes immediately apparent. For Sartre argues that in saying that a man is totally responsible for his own life, we are committed to saying that he has a responsibility for other people too. This argument takes a rather dubious form. It goes more or less as follows: If a man chooses anything, he chooses it *because he thinks it good*. Nothing can be good for us without being good for everyone; therefore what I choose, I am choosing for everyone. Another form of the same argument is that in choosing my life I am choosing a certain image of man, such as I think man ought to be. Therefore I am engaging the whole of mankind in my choice by saying to them all 'this is how you ought to be'. A choice, Sartre says, is the assertion of a value; and a value is necessarily universal. Subjectivity, from which Existentialism starts, entails only that each man chooses himself; but this necessarily means that he is choosing everyone else as well. At the end of the essay this argument becomes more explicit, and more explicitly Kantian. Sartre has defined Bad Faith, and characterised it as an attempt to escape from freedom. It is the use of a fake determinism as an excuse. 'The Spirit of Seriousness' is the name of a particular kind of Bad Faith, namely, that which tries to take refuge behind a supposedly absolute moral law, or scheme of ultimate values. Moralists are frequently guilty of this seriousness. Existentialism would avoid this; but it would also avoid another insidious kind of Bad Faith. For since my choice for myself involves a choice for others, Sartre argues that it is always appropriate to raise the question, 'What would happen if everyone did as you are doing?' If anyone answers this by saying 'but everyone won't', then he too is guilty of Bad Faith, for in fact he knows quite well, or could know if he chose, that choosing for himself *is* choosing for everyone.

Now at the end of the essay, Sartre seeks to show that *what* we choose, both for ourselves and others, must necessarily be freedom, if we are to choose in good faith. For freedom to make choices is part of the definition of man; and making choices, as he has already argued, entails asserting values; so all values, the very possibility of there being any values, depends on freedom. Therefore, as a matter of logic, we must value most highly that freedom which is the foundation of the possibility of value. There are various doubtful steps in this argument, on which I shall not comment. But the further corollary of it is that in choosing freedom for myself I must choose it for others; and thus that men, unless they take refuge in Bad Faith, must admit that they are committed to the freedom of others. Now this is a doctrine which is in many ways very attractive. The trouble is that it seems to be based on an ambiguity in the concept of universality. It may well be true that in explicitly judging something to be good we mean, as part of the judgment, that it is generally good, or good in any situation similar to that in which we are making the judgment.

→ It is part of the general condition for the use of language of any kind at all that we should assume a consistent use, within limits, for any element of the language. If this is to be called 'universalising', well and good, but there is nothing peculiar to the use of *value* words in this phenomenon. Quite different from this absolutely ubiquitous universalising would be the conscious adopting of a principle as a guide of universal application. Such an act of adoption would take, for instance, the verbal form 'It is a matter of principle that no one should . . .' or 'One ought always to . . .'. It seems perfectly obvious that we are not adopting such a principle every time we make a decision to act. We may be just acting for the best, as it seems to us, in a particular situation, and there might be no principle involved to which we should wish to commit ourselves, let alone one to which we should want to commit everyone in the world. It may be (though this is a doubtful step in itself) that in deciding what to do we think 'It would be best to do such and such' or even 'Such and such would be good' and it may be, further, that according to the conditions of the use of language already mentioned, if we did say 'such and such is good' we should have to be prepared to say that any exactly similar circumstances would also be described by us as good. But this by no means amounts to treating the course of action that we have this time chosen as something demanded by a universal principle. The mere universalisability of language is not strong enough to carry the weight of making us responsible in all our choices for legislating for the whole of humanity.

Sartre explicitly compares his doctrine with that of Kant, but criticises Kant for supposing that one could construct a morality purely formally and by appeal to universal principles. He was right, Sartre says, to assert that freedom wills itself and wills the freedom of others, but wrong to think that one formula, the categorical imperative, could define the scope of morality. It may well be true that Kant's theory is unduly schematic and formal. But at least Kant recognised, austerely, that a morally good decision must be explicitly subjected to the test of universalisation. The question must be asked: 'Is it rationally possible to envisage a world in which the principle I am about to act on is a universal law?' This question actually entails taking the ends, the goals, and the free voluntary actions of other people into account in making one's own decisions. And an alternative formulation of the categorical imperative is that one should do nothing which would mean treating another free human being merely as a means to one's own ends. Whether these two formulations are deducible from one another, or equivalent, as Kant seems to hold, need not concern us. The essential point is that, concrete or not, Kant's moral theory is firmly based on the law that, since the only ultimate good is the good free will, the free wills of others must never be overruled for some private and individual end. And he further held that if everyone had regard to this law, human ends would somehow fit with one another, and prove ultimately compatible with each other, in a 'Kingdom of Ends'.

That there is much which is incoherent or unclear about Kant's theory will not be denied. But it does contain a serious attempt to deal with the problem, which, as I have suggested already, seems to be at the heart of morality, namely, how one is to reconcile the free choices of one person with those of another equally free agent. Sartre, on the other hand, in the essay we are considering, merely *says* that in choosing freedom for myself I am choosing it for others, but does nothing to show how to avoid my freedom's clashing with that of others, or how to reconcile conflicting free choices. Moreover, as we have seen, he tries to show that there is a kind of logical necessity in my choosing freedom for myself and that this further logically entails my choosing it for others, since whatever I choose for myself I also choose for others. Neither of these logical points is enough to serve as the foundation of an ethical theory. Sartre contrasts the concrete and practical nature of his theory with the abstractions of Kant's. But in practice my choice of freedom for myself may often entail a lessening of freedom for others, and in this situation we can take no comfort from a reflection on the nature of language, or the need for consistency of use in such words as 'good' or 'free'. The fact is that neither in this essay, nor elsewhere, does Sartre give any convincing argument to show that we do, or indeed should, universalise our choices in any serious sense; nor does he show how it comes about that a choice of freedom for one, in any concrete situation, entails a choice of freedom for all. Moreover, in the *Critique of Dialectical Reason*[9] he explicitly denies that it makes sense to speak of treating humanity, or other human beings, as ends in themselves. Perhaps, too, it is worth noticing that, in the context of this particular essay, freedom means political and social freedom, so that a kind of liberal programme of increasing freedom for everyone might be derived from the doctrine outlined here, a Utilitarian programme of actual social and political reforms, such as would have pleased Mill.

But in two important respects such a doctrine cannot but be regarded as incompatible with the rest of Sartre's philosophy. First, any belief that there is in the world some absolutely valuable end, something which it must always be right to aim at, even other people's social or political emancipation, is precisely an example of the spirit of seriousness which, according to the doctrines of *Being and Nothingness*, vitiates the work of almost all moral philosophers, and is a kind of Bad Faith. Secondly, to suppose that we can, let alone that we must, take the mild humanitarian and altruistic view of other people suggested in the essay is completely in contradiction with the doctrines of *Being and Nothingness* concerning our inevitable relations with other people. If Sartre had claimed, in the essay, to have changed his mind, then we should have to accept these incompatibilities. But he made no such claim. On the contrary, he purported to be explaining his previous writings for the general public, and disabusing them of misconceptions about Existentialism in general. Unfortunately the doctrines of the essay are not, and cannot be thought to be, an exposition of the doctrines of *Being and Nothingness*; and since they are stated nowhere else, and were never defended by Sartre and indeed were repudiated by him, regretfully it seems that we must leave them. *Existentialism and Humanism* cannot be taken as a statement of Existentialist ethical theory in general, nor as a statement of Sartre's view in particular.

We must therefore turn back to *Being and Nothingness* to find out what answer he gave there to the fundamental ethical questions: 'How ought I to treat other people', and 'What is it which should be valued above everything else?' The answer to the second question is not different from that given in *Existentialism and Humanism*, but the consequences derived from it are far more depressing. Freedom is still the highest value, but each one of us alone has to try to face his freedom in his own choices, recognising that he is hemmed in on all sides by temptations to deny it, and attempts to deprive him of it. It is from this fact above all that the answer to our first question is to be derived, for there can be no doubt that in *Being and Nothingness* other people are the enemy, 'the original scandal of our existence'. We are committed to endless hostility, and our own freedom must often be won at the expense of sacrificing the will of another, who seeks to ensnare us. Let us look briefly at the picture of human relations in general presented by Sartre.

We have seen how, in *Being and Nothingness*, he describes the human situation in terms of hopes, plans, wishes, and aspirations. Consciousness, of its nature, is committed to some kind of *attempt upon* the world. Part of this attempt is to possess and control the world, to render it manageable and predictable. In the case of material objects, Beings-in-themselves, since they have fixed essences and are subject to discoverable laws, this attempt to organise and control the world is not entirely hopeless. But even here Sartre represents us as partially frustrated, of necessity. Even material objects have their own manner of existing which can seem recalcitrant and hostile. We may experience nausea when we survey what seems like the teeming, thick, viscous 'stickiness' of the world. Sartre thinks that such substances as treacle and honey are natural symbols of what we most hate in the world of things;

they represent the 'anti-value'. For, instead of being tidy and manageable, such that we can pick them up, manipulate them and define their boundaries, they are glutinous and spreading, neither liquid nor solid, possessing us by their stickiness, which clings to our fingers if we try to shake it off. We are naturally committed to feeling horror at this aspect of the world.

But if the world of things sometimes oppresses us with its refusal to conform to our categories and obey our control, the world of people is far more distressing. Other people are themselves free, and can therefore, by numerous deliberate means, escape our attempts to predict or control them. Our first effort, therefore, in our dealings with others, is to treat them as things, for, if they were things, if they lost their free power to act, we should at least be able to exercise a reasonable degree of control over them. We therefore label them as if they, like things, had unchanging essences. We say 'He is an Etonian', 'He is a stock-broker'; or we describe their characters, as though this was to describe essential essence of them. We say they are kind, lazy, vain, and so on, and attempt to predict their actions according to these descriptions. And so, once we have fixed them with a word, we treat them like other things, arguing about their probable behaviour by inductive methods. We tend to leave out of account the fact that they make plans and projects, frame intentions and form resolutions of their own. It is thus the *freedom* of other people which is an outrage to us, and we try to overcome it by pretending it does not exist. We have seen already how the fact that other people treat us in this way impinges on us, and determines our consciousness of ourselves, in a world surrounded by others. The concrete relations between one person and another which follow from these basic facts about our existence in the world are described by Sartre in chapter three of the third part of *Being and Nothingness*. He says: 'While I attempt to free myself from the hold of the Other, the Other is trying to free himself from mine; while I seek to enslave the Other, the Other seeks to enslave me. We are by no means dealing with unilateral relations with an object-in-itself, but with reciprocal and moving relations. . . . descriptions of concrete behaviour must therefore be envisaged within the perspective of *conflict*. Conflict is the original meaning of being-for-others.[10] Here there is clearly a reflection of Hegel's notorious doctrine of master and slave. Hegel had held that our self-consciousness was real only in so far as it recognised an echo and a reflection of itself in the existence of another; but that out of this fact sprang an inevitable opposition between myself and the other. For I aim to have as an integral cause of my self-consciousness a being who is only this and nothing else, who exists for nothing else but for my ends. Thus I struggle ceaselessly to reduce the other to the status of a slave. It seems fair, therefore, to describe Sartre's doctrine of our relationship with other people as Hegelian.

But one can go further; the Hegelian conflict in which we are locked is essentially hopeless. For what I want to get hold of is the other's freedom. It is of no use to me to possess him if he is not still a free human being when he is mine. If I killed him I would in a way possess him, but since he would no longer be free this would not satisfy me. He would have escaped me in the end, by dying. On the other hand, if he is still free, then he necessarily escapes me. I cannot control what he thinks, or plans to do. A free conscious being cannot be possessed. It is this which ensures that there can be no such thing, for instance, as a wholly satisfactory love affair. For though we want to turn the person we love into a thing we can control, with no freedom, yet we also want to be freely loved by this person. It would not satisfy us if the person we loved *had* to love us, if love were, for instance, the result of a potion. It has to be his choice to love us. Yet it is just his ability to choose which is a threat to us and which we want to destroy. Sartre thinks that in love there are just three patterns of behaviour which are possible, and that we shall inevitably adopt one or the other, but all are unsatisfactory. We may lapse into indifference; we may turn to masochism, which is to aim to become a thing ourselves, to be used and controlled by the other; or we may become sadists, which means trying to possess the other by violence. There is nothing possible except one of the three; and conflict is the inevitable basis of the relation. It is from the inevitability of the conflict that Sartre derives the consequence, plainly stated in the *Critique of Dialectical Reason*, that we can in no way adopt other people as ends in themselves. We cannot suppose that Sartre gave up the whole of his view of our relation with others when he wrote the essay *Existentialism and Humanism*. We must therefore regard the suggested ethical philosophy contained in that essay as an aberration.

What, then, are the possibilities for ethics? First we must notice an unresolved contradiction in *Being and Nothingness*, which Sartre does not pay enough attention to. How can we reconcile the belief that we are absolutely free to choose whatever life we want, to be what we want, with the belief that in our dealings with others we are committed entirely to an unending conflict from which there is no escape? It seems that these two beliefs cannot be wholly reconciled, and that this constitutes at least part of the difficulty with which Sartre is faced in constructing any ethical theory at all. If ethics, as we have supposed, is concerned with the fitting together of the interests and choices of one person with those of another, there is no way into the subject at all if our aim is *necessarily* to dominate the other person and subordinate his freedom to our own.

There is, moreover, another equally powerful objection to the construction of an ethical theory, which we have already noticed. We are debarred, on pain of Bad Faith, from asserting that anything is absolutely valuable. The particular kind of Bad Faith involved here is the 'Spirit of Seriousness'. The belief that some things are good in themselves, and the belief that some things are always good because their consequences are, absolutely, desirable are both equally expressions of this spirit. Both naturalism, in the form of the belief that happiness or pleasure is what, as a matter of fact, everybody values; and non-naturalism, in the form of a belief in an absolute and transcendent system of values, must equally be abandoned. Of a morality based on such beliefs, Sartre says: 'It has obscured all its goals in order to free itself from anguish. Man pursues being blindly by hiding from himself the free project which is this pursuit. He makes himself such that he is *waited for* by all the tasks placed along his way. Objects are mute demands, and he is nothing in himself but the passive obedience to these demands.'[11] Any theoretical morality appears to lead to the one thing which is hostile to morality's very existence, namely, passive obedience.

We may ask then what task is left for the moral philosopher. He may, presumably, without harm, devote himself to analysing the language of morals. For example, it is possible to state, analytically, that men assign values to whatever they please; and such an analysis of ethical propositions would be a philosophical exercise, it is true. But to offer such an analysis is both to take a short way with ethics, and to run the risk of seeming to trivialise the subject. Sartre would hardly be content with the brief few pages allotted to ethics by Ayer in *Language, Truth and Logic*. Whatever his final views about ethics might be, we would not expect them to be identical with the jaunty simplifications of the logical positivists.

We may summarise Sartre's position at the end of *Being and Nothingness* as follows: First of all men are free: 'For human reality, to be is to choose oneself.' Choosing oneself entails assigning values to things, and this we do simply by regarding some goals as worth pursuing, others not. To evaluate something, to say that it is good or worth pursuing, is not to describe it; it is to set it up as something to be aimed at. But to say of something that it is to be aimed at is to say that it is ideal, and ideals are, by definition, unattainable. That the good or the perfect is unattainable seems to Sartre self-evidently true. For anything attainable would not be such that we would seek it as an end. It is because of the impossibility of attaining what is morally valuable that, according to Sartre, moral philosophers have been in the habit of saying both that the property of goodness existed unconditionally, and also that it did not exist at all. Arguments about God's existence, he thinks, also spring from this fact. For every human being, as we have seen, forms the project of becoming somehow complete, *massif*, entirely, through and through, what he is not. But if he ever did become something in itself, with the completeness and solidity he desires, he would thereby lose the essentially human characteristic, constitutive of his consciousness, of being empty and without essence. So 'God' is the name given to that impossible conjunction of properties which we should all most like to have, the conjunction of consciousness with *massif* being, such as only Beings-in-themselves possess. 'Every human reality is a passion in that it projects losing itself . . . to constitute the In-Itself which escapes contingency . . . the *Ens causa sui*, which religions call God. Thus the passion of man is the reverse of that of Christ, for man loses himself as man in order that God may be born. But the idea of God is contradictory and we lose ourselves in vain. Man is a useless passion.'[12]

But despite being blocked on all sides, by the need to avoid Bad Faith on the one hand, and by the necessity of human conflict on the other, Sartre holds that some kind of morality must necessarily exist. He says: 'Value is everywhere and nowhere. . . . It is simply lived as the concrete meaning of that lack which makes my present being. Thus reflective consciousness can properly be called moral consciousness, since it cannot arise without at the same time disclosing values.' In choosing for ourselves, as we have seen, we are 'disclosing values', since we choose what we think worth choosing, by definition. So, since men are free, and must choose if they live at all, they are necessarily moral beings. Accepting values from another rather than knowingly and deliberately adopting one's own values in choice, indeed, accepting any general rules for behaviour, must be Bad Faith. The moralist's advice seems to be simply to avoid Bad Faith; for since we are free, we ought to realise that we are, and not evade our freedom. But such a morality, it must be said, is entirely negative. It has no positive content, so far. All we know is that morality consists in the attempt to isolate oneself, to escape the influence of one's environment, and heroically to take full responsibility for what it is that one does. There is something of a familiar and not unattractive ethos here. Anything is better than making excuses, or trying to duck out of responsibility; the only obligation is to face one's situation, no matter what it is. Moral man is sincere man; immorality is phoniness. At the very end of *Being and Nothingness*, there is a hint of how such a moral theory might be given some content. For Sartre says that once the moral agent has realised that he is himself the source of all values 'his freedom

49

will become conscious of itself and reveal itself in anguish, as the unique source of values, and the emptiness by which the world exists'. The possibility of acting must be realised in the context of a concrete situation, where the agent is surrounded by actual other people. The moral question for each man is, then, to what extent he can escape from the bonds of his particular situation, and how much responsibility he will take for creating, act by act, the world in which he lives. Sartre promises to discuss these questions in another book written, he says 'on an ethical level'. But such a book was never written, as we shall see.

A further hint is contained in a footnote to a passage we have already noted. In the discussion of human relations, Sartre has concluded that in all relationships one is bound to fall into either masochism or sadism. To this conclusion, he adds the following note: 'These considerations do not exclude the possibility of an ethics of deliverance and salvation. But this can be achieved only after a radical conversion which we cannot discuss here.'[13] The radical conversion must be a change of plan, it must give rise to a new way for each human being to project himself upon the world and to choose his own life. It must give him a new vision of his possible life with other human beings, and one which does not necessarily end in frustration. For we have seen that, though in the essay *Existentialism and Humanism* Sartre was anxious to rebut the charge of the critics of Existentialism that it was a philosophy of despair, yet from the end of *Being and Nothingness* there is nothing offered to a clear-sighted and honest man except an endlessly frustrated attempt to break out of the deterministic circle of the only fundamental attitudes to other people which are possible for him. However much he is said to be free to choose himself and his life, what he chooses, in so far as it affects others, will always be either sadism, masochism, or indifference. Individual freedom comes to look like nothing but freedom either to face the disagreeable facts of one's situation, or to cover them up by the evasions of Bad Faith. Morality consists in choosing the former, the heroic, course.

In fact we know that the radical conversion came and was the conversion to Marxism which is set out in the *Critique of Dialectical*

Reason. The struggle between one human being and another, which in *Being and Nothingness* arose from a psychological necessity derived from the nature of consciousness itself, has become, in the *Critique*, an impersonal Hobbesian struggle of all against all, caused, not by psychological but by economic necessity. It is *scarcity* which brings about the conflict, and scarcity, though it is part of the only world we know, is a contingent feature of the world, and we can conceive that one day it might be eliminated. If it were eliminated, then human relations would change. It is therefore now possible to work towards the removal of scarcity from the world, as a goal. The society in which the struggle is unchecked is called the *collective*, and the condition of its members is the condition of *seriality*. In this condition, people are scarcely human, for each is just a generalised man — bound by his needs and by the desire to get more for himself; and any man is, in this aspect, interchangeable with any other. In such a society the only motive is greed, and men are mere units. There is no community of interests, and no one has any particular role. The way out of the serial society is in the formation of the *group*. The essential feature of the group is that there should be an absolute identity of will between the members. The situation in which the group characteristically emerges is that of revolution, where two or more people become one person, since they have an absolutely common project, to overthrow a regime which has been seen to be intolerable to each of them. What one person wills is literally identical with what the other wills. After the revolution, it is the aim of humanity to avoid relapsing, in any part of political or social life, into the chaotic and deterministic condition of seriality.

Even from this crude summary, it will be seen how very far from Existentialism Sartre's radial conversion has taken him. Indeed, in *The Problem of Method*,[14] which prefaces the *Critique*, he explicitly states that there can, in the present age, be no philosophy that is not Marxist. Marxism is, for the time being, the dominant philosophy. Existentialism is a minor ideology, which must be seen as making a contribution to thought, within a Marxist framework. The contribution which it can make is to render Marxism concrete. He complains that Marxism has become a kind of dry dogmatic orthodoxy, with its conclusions derived automatically from certain unexamined and accepted premises. Existentialism could 'interiorise' Marxism, by displaying, in their concrete and actually experienced forms, the various elements in the Marxist account of the world. It could describe, from the inside, the Group, the Revolution, the Labour of man, the actual *praxis*, or action, in which men intervene in the world of things. Sartre here seems to envisage the peculiar virtues of Existentialism being brought to bear on Marxist theory, to give it new life, the concentration, that is on *what it is like* for the individual to be in the world he is in, how he will feel in choosing to support the Revolution, how this decision will come to him, as an individual. Unfortunately, there is very little of this humanising influence to be seen in the *Critique*. But, more important, even if Sartre had fulfilled his promise to 'interiorise' Marxism, this would still have been the end of Existentialism as a kind of philosophy. For the role assigned to Existentialism is at best a minor and essentially a *literary* role. The task of interiorising is quite distinct from any kind of theory-building. It is the decoration, perhaps, which is put on, after the house is built. The rendering of the Marxist choice concrete, the presentation of the *vérité vécue* of the revolutionary spirit — all this could be done better by a novelist or playwright or film-maker than by a philosopher. If an Existentialist undertook such a task, he might very well have a moral *purpose*, but that is very different from having a moral philosophy of his own. At least for Sartre, there can be no doubt that, just as the individual of *Being and Nothingness* has been swallowed up in the Group of the *Critique*, so Existentialism itself has been swallowed up in Marxism.

V. CONCLUSION

It is time now to see what general conclusions can be drawn from our consideration of Kierkegaard, Heidegger, and Sartre. There can be no doubt that all three of them were deeply interested in ethical questions, that is, in trying to provide a theoretical and not merely a practical answer to the question 'How ought people to live?' And this preoccupation with ethics, the treating of all philosophy as ultimately leading up to an answer to the ethical question, may be fairly taken to be a common characteristic of all Existentialist thinkers. For an Existentialist, what philosophical beliefs you hold determines the actual way in which you live your life. And, as we saw at the beginning, the aim of philosophy for an Existentialist, is not to provide a pure, disinterested statement of truth, but to free people from their illusions. Thus, not only do ethical questions emerge in Existentialist philosophy as the most important questions to which all others are merely preliminary but, going along with this, the whole aim of a philosopher must have a moral purpose.

So much could be agreed. But at this stage difficulties begin to appear. For we have seen that the great illusion from which people are to be freed is the illusion of determinism. The blindness which these philosophers aim to cure is a man's blindness to his own freedom. *That man is a free agent* is the fundamental doctrine of Existentialism. But the existence of freedom is not a *doctrine* to be questioned; it is taken to be a natural *fact*, which, if we are not corrupted by fear or prejudice, we can simply experience as true in our own lives. It is no more sensible to deny man's freedom than to deny that he is capable of distinguishing colours, or of counting. That a man is free means that he is free to choose what to do. Choice consists in his looking at his situation, and seeing how he personally is going to intervene in it. I cannot choose for you, because if you act on my decision, then thereby it becomes your decision. Just as it is impossible, logically, that I should walk your steps, or feel your pain, or, in the same way as you do, raise your eyebrows, so it is impossible that I should make your decision. If you say you were acting only in accordance with my will, this is an evasion. In fact, if you would only acknowledge it, the decision was, of necessity, yours. Ethics must therefore be concerned with individuals, and how they make their choices. It is thus that the insistence upon human freedom leads directly to the other great concern of Existentialist thought, namely, subjectivity. Choices must be made by each man for himself. So they must be described as what each *individual* plans as he looks out at the world from his own personal angle. He cannot be told by anyone else what is to be valued highly and what is not, nor, therefore, what is to be done and what is not. We ascribe values to things ourselves, whether we mean to or not. If I choose to pursue a certain course of action, then in so doing I *am* evaluating. Systems of rules are of their nature impersonal. To live according to such a system is to fail to face the facts of individual freedom and responsibility. Pretending to be able to teach others how to behave is like the sophists' pretence, which Socrates was concerned to expose, the pretence that the *truth* could be taught. If we adhere to customary or code-like moral systems we are as much deluded as the people who paid the sophists money to tell them philosophical truths. To free someone from illusions, then, one must make him realise his total isolation. He is wholly responsible for creating his own world, in living the way he does.

It is easy to see how this kind of view may degenerate into absurdity. It may well develop into a view of life in which absolutely everything that a man does is to be interpreted as a sign of some real decision or real evaluation he has made, so that, for example, the particular manner in which he leans up against the bar may be taken to express his whole world-picture; his deciding to shave or to grow a beard is as essential a choice of himself, as is his decision to join the army or the police force. If choosing freely for oneself is the highest value, the free choice to wear red socks is as valuable as the free choice to murder one's father or sacrifice oneself for one's friend. Such a belief is ridiculous. It tends, moreover, to show itself in a kind of vague wordless acceptance of *everything* as deeply significant. What is so significant about his standing hour after hour leaning against the bar? The answer is that he is thereby choosing what to be; he is living out his choice to be a man who stands hour after hour leaning against the bar. As long as he knows what he is doing, then his choice is morally unexceptionable, indeed is morally commendable. The tendency of Existentialist thought to provoke in the reader the desire to deflate the whole thing is most manifest at this point. What the Existentialists are maintaining, we feel inclined to say, is that people sometimes have to decide what to do, and that they are capable of doing so. At a commonsense level, we never doubted this for a moment. At a philosophical level the problems raised by saying that man is free are enormous, and have occupied philosophers for centuries. But about these problems the Existentialists have almost nothing to say. For they simply believe that it is self-evident that men are free, and that we learn this fact directly from experience. So the doctrine of freedom seems obvious at one level and unsatisfactory at another, and, as we have suggested before, exaggerated at either level.

We are *not* in fact free to choose absolutely anything. To accept, for example, the categories under which we normally describe the world is *not* a free voluntary decision. We learn these categories as we learn to talk, and to see the world otherwise would be in many cases impossible. It seems to me that there are further features of our life which are not a matter of choice. For instance, we do not choose to prefer pleasure to pain. Despite Sartre's arguments, we may well deny that we at any rate always choose what to feel, or how to react emotionally to the world. In all these ways the extreme subjectivism and the extreme libertarianism of the existentialists seem equally unacceptable.

Besides leading to absurdity, the kind of view we have been considering has serious consequences for ethics. If ethics is concerned with the manner in which men, as rational creatures, think about their own behaviour, and attempt to solve their problems and adapt themselves to one another in society, then it must be possible to formulate certain general rules either about what people do in fact think, or about what they do in fact hold valuable. From here it is only a short step to regarding some types of action as generally to be avoided, others as generally to be pursued; or to holding some types of motives as generally to be preferred to others. But such reliance, at whatever level of discourse, upon general rules or principles is taken by Existentialism to be a denial of freedom. The only general law of ethics must be to avoid general laws. Just as, for Kierkegaard, religion became degenerate, indeed ceased to be religion at all, as soon as it was institutionalised, so morality for any Existentialist ceases to be morality the moment it is encapsulated in principles of conduct. There is value in both these positions. To insist that religion is a private matter, that merely observing certain forms has nothing to do with it, has always been the religious reformer's role. And doubtless in the same way, there is value in issuing a warning against the rigid and unimaginative view that we must always do our duty, and we have only to think a little to find out what our duty is. That there is just one right thing which is waiting to be done in each situation is moral formalism, and might lead to the view that having satisfied the formal requirements, there is nothing else that can be demanded of a man. To 'interiorise' morals, to render them both concrete and personal in contrast to such formalism is something which is well worth doing. And this is what Existentialist moralists have done. But without *some* element of objectivity, without *any* criterion for preferring one scheme of values to another, except the criterion of what looks most attractive to oneself, there cannot in fact be any morality at all, and moral theory must consist only in the assertion that there is no morality. Kierkegaard may be thought to have rejected all that is normally meant by religion in trying to purge religion of its bogus elements. In the same way one may suspect that morality itself has disappeared, and with it the possibility of moral theory, in the efforts of those who wish to clear out the worthless, the insincere and the non-genuine from the theories of moral philosophers. It cannot be doubted that the existence of Existentialist philosophy has had a profound effect both on the writing of moral philosophy, in making it more concrete and realistic, and on morality itself as actually practised. But it is far more doubtful whether it can be claimed that there is any *direct* contribution to philosophy which should be described as Existentialist ethics. For the demands of philosophy, exactness, objectivity, and the attempt to say what is true, are the very demands which Existentialism is committed, on principle, to rejecting. Perhaps we must conclude that Existentialism, as a way of thinking, is more naturally suited to express itself in novels, plays, films, and other unargued statements of how the world is. We have seen some of the characteristic features of these expressions. It seems that to be attracted by Existentialism is to be attracted by a mood. When it comes to serious thought, one may find, as Sartre did, that it is necessary to cast off the mood and start again.

NOTES

1. *Kierkegaard's Concluding Unscientific Postscript*, translated from the Danish by D. F. Swenson, with Introduction and Notes by W. Lowrie (Princeton University Press and O.U.P., 1941), pp. 118, 119.
2. Op. cit., pp. 116, 117.
3. Op. cit., pp. 178, 183.
4. [L'Être et le Néant] *Being and Nothingness: An Essay on Phenomenological Ontology*, translated by Hazel E. Barnes (Methuen, 1957), p. 246.
5. [Esquisse d'une théorie des émotions] *Sketch for a Theory of the Emotions*, translated by P. Mairet (Methuen, 1962), p. 31.
6. [L'Existentialisme est un humanisme] *Existentialism and Humanism*, translated by P. Mairet (Methuen, 1948), p. 64.
7. *Being and Nothingness*, pp. 59, 60.
8. Op. cit., p. 55.
9. *Critique de la Raison dialectique* (Gallimard: Paris, 1960).
10. *Being and Nothingness*, p. 364.
11. Op. cit., p. 626.
12. Op. cit., p. 615.
13. Op. cit., p. 412 n.
14. [Question de Méthode] *The Problem of Method*, translated by Hazel E. Barnes (New York, 1964).

BIBLIOGRAPHY

I. Selection of Standard Texts in Translation

Buber, Martin. *I and Thou* (Edinburgh, 1937).
  Between Man and Man (London, 1947).
Heidegger, Martin. *Existence and Being* (London, 1949).
  Being and Time (London, 1962).
Kierkegaard, Søren. *Concluding Unscientific Postscript* (Princeton and O.U.P., 1941).
  Philosophical Fragments (Princeton and O.U.P., 1941).
Sartre, Jean-Paul. *Existentialism and Humanism* (London, 1948).
  Being and Nothingness (London, 1957).
  Nausea (London, 1962).
  Sketch for a Theory of the Emotions (London 1962).

II. Studies in Existentialist Thought

Lowrie, W. *A Short Life of Kierkegaard* (London, 1943).
Jeanson, F. *Le Problème Moral et la Pensée de Sartre* (Paris, 1947).
Murdoch, I. *Sartre, Romantic Rationalist* (Cambridge, 1953).
Copleston, F. C. *Contemporary Philosophy* (London, 1956).
Roubiczek, P. *Existentialism, For and Against* (Cambridge, 1964).
Warnock, M. *The Philosophy of Sartre* (London, 1965).
Manser, A. *Sartre* (London, 1966).